GW01465402

Tattoo Me

Pamela Greene

very best wishes
Pamela
11. 4. 2002

SUMMER PALACE PRESS

First published in 2002 by

Summer Palace Press
Cladnageeragh, Kilbeg, Kilcar, County Donegal, Ireland

ARTS
COUNCIL
of Northern Ireland

Printed by Nicholson & Bass Ltd.

A catalogue record for this book is available
from the British Library

ISBN 0 9535912 6 3

for
my father and mother

Acknowledgments

Versions of some of the poems in this book have appeared in:

HU; Poetry Ireland Review (1996); *Sunday Tribune; Fortnight; The White Page,* edited by Joan McBreen for Salmon Press (1999); *Down at the Millennium* (2000); *heresay* and *Full Moon.*

Biographical Note
Pamela Greene was born in Belfast in 1951. She graduated from the Queen's University, Belfast, with a First Class Honours Degree in Spanish Language and Literature. After graduating, she lived in Marseilles before returning to Belfast where she undertook a three-year apprenticeship to qualify as a solicitor. She currently practises law in Belfast. She has participated in several fringe readings at the Belfast Festival at Queen's, including, in 1997, a live performance installation entitled 'Transfluences'. She has read at various venues throughout Ireland and participated in Poetry Ireland 'Introductions' in 2001. A pamphlet, *heartland,* was published by Lapwing Press in 1998.

CONTENTS

Angel

My mother dreamed of being an archangel
and through long winter nights
fashioned herself snowy white wings
from hens' feathers sewn to a chicken-wire frame
and a sword out of a length of rusted metal
beaten painfully into shape.

By spring she was ready.
Each evening she would stand at our garden gate,
sword held close across her chest,
wings outspread.
Only the good shall enter here, she'd say,
barring entrance to anyone who called.

My father lay back in his chair,
filling and refilling his pipe.
It'll pass, he'd say softly, *it'll pass*,
but summer was long in coming
and when I looked into my mother's eyes
I saw fear, black as a raven, behind her watchfulness.

He came to our gate at midsummer,
the stranger, with eyes of peacock blue,
his throat garlanded with flowers.
Lay down your sword, he said to my mother,
my heart is pure,
you and yours have nothing to fear from me.

I alone saw a veil of mist descend
over my mother's eyes
as she lowered her sword
and in silence stood aside to let him in.
I alone saw the small birds, colourful as ribbons,
hanging lifeless from his belt.

His presence filled our whole house
and for a while there was music, laughter and song,
although my mother's face was troubled
as she busied herself in the kitchen,
her wings setting dust motes
dancing in the sunlight.

Come, sit with me, he said to my mother,
patting the empty chair beside him.
Quietly she sat,
her wings trembling.

Without a word
he stretched out his huge hand,
grasped her breast
and crushed it between his fingers,
the sudden roar of his laughter a thousand rooks
encircling us in a black feathered frenzy.

Woman, he said, *it was yourself invited me in.*
In that instant I saw my mother, small as a wren,
hanging with bloodied feathers
from the loop of his belt,
her wings broken,
sword bent and useless.

Winter approaches.
The house is quiet and forlorn without my mother.
I am fashioning my own wings from feathers
gathered from black birds
while my father sleeps, restless as a child.

These days, fear crouches in my throat.

Rainy Days before the Solstice

I go shuffle-shoulder among strangers,
smelling the intimate familiarity of their rain-wetness,
swept along by them through the city's granite streets,
an Atlantic expanse of greys and browns.

Clouds squeeze my head and I give up on thought.
Occasionally a smile, a laugh, a flash of beautiful eyes
washes up on my hungry shore,
an exotic flotsam that tantalizes
but resubmerges before I can lay claim.

I try to name the rains
but cannot get beyond downpour
through deluge, torrent, cloudburst, drizzle, mizzle, mist.

I read somewhere that the Inuit have sixty-four names for snow
(one-hundred-and-thirty-nine according to my daughter)
and I am suddenly in their world
listening to the howl of snow,
its polar-bear weight crushing me to the ground,
the smell of ice rank in my nostrils.
My heart contracts with cold
and I bless the lord that I can only come up with seven names for rain.

Four more days until the solstice.
I'll build an ark and start my journey,
upwards,
to the light.

Frances in the Garden

With a furious concentration my grandmother
weeds among the vegetable rows,
her small body gathered into itself like a tightly-folded sheet.

She never smiles.
I think she keeps them locked away
in the small box on her bedside table,
to be taken out,
dusted and polished
for wear on Sundays or when visitors call.

When she stands to draw breath,
I am afraid she will face out the sun again
and make it change course
or send it retreating behind a cloud,

but not today,

today she runs twisted fingers through wind-loosed hair,
pulls her cardigan taut across the flat planes of her chest,
tugs her disobedient skirt back into place
and kneels to weed a new row,
order restored.

A sudden scream.
My grandmother staggers awkwardly to her feet,
her wellington boot filling to the brim with blood.

Together we stare at the shard of glass in her leg
as if it were the most ordinary thing,
while a smile, quick as a shadow,
passes across her lips
momentarily darkening the summer garden sun.

Waiting for You

I have put on a Japanese face,
combed camellia oil into my hair
and poured green tea into two tiny cups
fragile as rice paper.

I am kneeling on the tatami matting
in my blue and green kimono
with obi of crimson,
your favourite colours.

To pass the time, I paint ideographs
on a silk screen;
your name,
over and over,
as though in naming you
I could capture the youness of you.

And if I could recreate you, flesh and bone,
would you be as you were
or would you be a stranger
because my memory has failed
to preserve you perfectly?

How long the night is.
I sit with hands resting one in the other
as you taught me,
though decorum was never an easy lesson.

The wind rises.
You will not come now
and tomorrow the cherry blossom
will shed its petals, one by one.

The Winter House

wraps its walls around me
and with frosted breath, whispers
of the child in the attic
with the doll she calls her sister,
singing *one for sorrow, two for joy* as she combs its flaxen hair.

The winter house opens the doors of its largest room,
emptiness spilling out with a chorus of sighs.
In its windows and mirrors I see reflected
a sad-eyed child in a bridal dress,
a circlet of withered daisies in her autumn hair.
She is dancing a slow waltz with an invisible partner,
the only music, the metronome of rain dripping from the eaves.

I look beyond the windows, across the fields of sedge
to the trees where the magpies are nesting.
One for sorrow, two for joy, the winter house murmurs,
everything comes to solitude in the end.

Somewhere on an upper floor, a child sings a lullaby
and the winter house hums the short refrain.

The rooms begin spinning slowly like prayer wheels
as I watch the birches in the garden wake from sleep.

The winter house gathers me gently to its heart,
but I need to be unwalled
in a place where memories do not dwell.

Circle of Smoke and Feathers

Walking to work, I passed a man smoking a cigar
who reminded me of another man, also smoking a cigar,
in the amphitheatre,
in Orange,
where we listened to opera under a summer moon
and watched a pigeon swoop and soar with the voices,
its flight weaving the night with feathers.

I half-remembered a story of a woman who opened
the windows in a hall where a concert was to be held
and how hundreds of birds
came roller-coastering across the sky
to fly in through the windows as one,
their song raising the roof high above her head.

When I got to work
I found three pigeons huddled together in the library,
their throats silent,
the smell of their fear pungent as cigar smoke.

Madeleine

I heard Madeleine's laughter before we met.
It was as if a window
in that dark-shadowed flat in Marseilles
had been thrown suddenly open to the sun.

And then Madeleine herself,
vibrant as a Mozart sonata.
I'd loved her instantly,
her energy stirring me out of a deep sleep,
her voice a helter-skelter ride of excitement
on a language I did not understand.

But when I first saw those six numbers
cut unevenly into the soft flesh of her inner arm
I went running back to the shadows to hide,
too late,
from the still bright blue of that ink.

My children have never met Madeleine.
I need to tell them of her
and of the invisible numbers marking us all.

My Light in the Darkness

I wanted it easy;
wanted to lead my tottering mother unbuffeted
and unassailed into the hospital's tower,
but a stormy day and a surfeit of people
almost blew us off course
though we came finally to that maze of corridors
where the elderly nod on plastic seats,
their mumblings an endless mantra,
and the sick lie on trolleys, blank-eyed and paper-pale.

I hate the bright cheerful colours, the muzak.
My mother is oblivious to both,
her head nodding to her own concerto
as we wait and wait and wait.

Beside us an old man farts,
his eyes milky-white and tearful.
I am suddenly afraid
and would reach for my mother's hand
except I am the grown-up now,
and it is she who reaches out for me
trusting that I will know what to do.

My ever and forever mother,
body-scarred,
mind full of black holes.

Looking at her, I wonder whether the shift
in my own body's chemistry has already begun,
whether my memories have started to vanish.
I wonder if I have the courage
to face whatever will come.

Flight

My daughter and I in a blue air afternoon
pass beyond boundaries to the heart of Mourne.
Our feet, tentative at first,
soon discover a new freedom
in this gloriously unpeopled place
where mountains tremble
and sky is awhirl with light.

A solitary raven teaches us flight;
for an age we ride the thermals,
swooping among crags,
sculling the heather,
racing the sun.

My daughter, joyous and unafraid,
flies far beyond me higher than sound,
way up into the midnight blue silence.

I do not fear that her wings will melt
and send her crashing to the ground,
for she wears the feathers of owls
and she knows that women
always return safely to the earth.

The Watcher
after the painting by Paul Henry

He calls her the watcher.
But what if she is blind and cannot see
the turbulent greys and greens before her eyes,
feels instead through booted feet
the rock vibrate,
hears the minute crumbling of the island's edge
under the ceaseless suck and surge of sea?

He has placed her hand by her face,
its purpose hidden.
Perhaps she tastes the day upon her fingers,
salt-bitter, moist and cool,
or seals her lips
to prevent her voice being stolen by gulls
whose screams are splintered on the wind.

He has painted her dress red,
a brave defiant colour in a mute land.
But if she were blind
then red could be the grease of lanolin,
the smell of turf,
the roughness of the yarn against
the softness of her skin.

He calls her the watcher.
But what if she is simply praying to the sea
that she will one day leave this windwild place?

Currach

Adrift, I feel the weight of his body guiding
me over the swollen waves, the language
of his hands turning me into the throat of the wind.

My body is rounded as the belly of a woman
heavy with child. I am a skin taut-fitted
over ash ribs. He wears me closer

than a lover, has adorned me with pitch
black as the absence of moon on water.
Through me he hears the running of shoals,

sees fish darting, quicksilver,
among kelp beds. I let him guide me
with his salt-cracked hands, his silent

listening for the roar of rocks. It is nothing
to me whether we reach shore
or disappear into the infinite grey.

Pinto

He is the Indian pony,
high-stepping
out of the woods
to circle me at a distance,
wary of sudden gesture
or movement,
uncertain of my intent.

With tentative step
he approaches,
ready to run should
my voice blow a cold wind
or fall harshly upon him.

He allows me to take hold
of his tangled mane,
his sweet, warm breath on my skin
reminding me
of our once, long-ago connection.

Gentling him,
he looks beyond me
to distances I cannot see.

Winter is over.
I must fold away his blanket of wool.

Lacelight

Where light becomes shade
there is an old woman on a straight-backed chair
sewing lace stretched taut on its frame;
a white hunger for love.

Beyond her oak door, the sun crushes breath
from the alley-way, its ochre walls
and shuttered windows echoing
the early morning's gossip, whispers and laughter.

At midday the sun fists open her door
to find her sleeping, unseeing,
as it pokes through her lacework, patterning
the earthen floor with the madness of fish.

At four the church bells rouse her fingers,
brides to the bridegroom, they go dancing
to the lace to weave joy and sorrow
with the unravelling thread of her life.

Silently she sits, feeling through bones of bird
the fading sun, feeling through leathered feet
the earth's great plates shift
in the way of lovers who have known each other too well.

In the moon's light lace swirls around her,
whiter than sea foam.
She is the black rock on which waves break.

That Day We Went to the Rijksmuseum

people nodded, pointed at you
and said you were van Gogh,
and for a moment it was him I saw
in the flame of your hair,
the wintergreen of your eyes,
the sharp angles of your face

but I knew they were mistaken
for I have felt the touch of your hands
and I know that yours is a different art,
your colours too subtle for the unknowing eye
though you also created star-spun nights,
rook-wild days,
and your gifts were sunflowers and irises
brilliant in yellows and blue.

Van Gogh or not,
you taught me the colours of touch.
In your unsevered ear, I whisper my name.

Stairway between Lives

The hedgerows are aflame, my father used to say,
pointing at the fuschia,
tiny fires, tiny fires.

I want opera, he'd say,
filling our house with huge music,
coloured all colours, liquid as light.

Do onto others as you'd have them do onto you, he'd say,
looking at me over half-moon glasses,
his eyes smiling.

My mother told me of the long flight of steps from the hotel;
bleached by the sun, they were the colour of bone.
And how she could not look over her shoulder at the hyacinth sea
for fear she might run and hurl herself headlong
into its tumbling waves.

She told me she kept telling him it would be all right,
his pain a band of steel around her own heart,
her hands helpless, as his grasped the armrests of his wheelchair,
knuckles white with fear.

She told me how she walked backwards down that flight of steps,
guiding his chair,
not daring to think of a future without him.

Snowfall

spectacularly white
as though her mother had stepped outdoors
just before dawn
shaken out her best linen tablecloths
letting them settle softly
on the fields
horizon to horizon
no sound
just the shadow of a loop of birds

More than the Sum of the Parts

I buried my son without his eyes.
How will he ever find his way home?

I buried my son without his tongue.
How will he cry out for me when he is afraid?

I buried my son without his heart,
his small, ungrown heart.
How will he fill the hole in his chest where love made its home?

I buried my son without his hands.
How will he reach out to me to pull him from danger,
hold him safe and secure?

I buried my son without his head.
How will I recognize him again
when I do not know if his spirit wears his face or walks free?

Lord, tell me what it is I have buried;
the broken, invaded body that lies silent and empty
surely cannot be my beloved son.

Dream of Stone

Bring me back a stone, he said, *let that be your gift.*

Restless in her bed
she dreams of skin that does not smell of turf;
she dreams of fingers, soft as swansdown,
that paint her body with crescent moons
and antlered heads
and beckon her to the rock-strewn shore
to walk the length of night.

With outstretched hands she bids the waves be still
to listen to the song of stones beneath the deep water.

From the seabed she plucks a blue stone
the colour of a Himalayan poppy.
Holding its smooth shape to her cheek
she sees the two bodies entwined,
their skin patterned with sand and kelp,
starfish in their eyes.

The sea rises to reclaim them
while the wind strums fretfully the ribs of a whale,
the sound high and quivering
like an overtuned harp.

Waves wash the bodies clean,
revealing the eyes of one, blue as her lover's eyes,
blue as the stone.

She wakens to the sea's surge,
sand on her pillow,
the blue stone held tight in her hand.

Longing

She could be a roe deer standing
still as silence
in the long grasses of dawn,
her skin a fine silk over willow bones,
her eyes holding him as though
he were the hunted.

It would thrill him to his soul
to see her turn
leaping through the skeins of mist,
an elemental creature
momentarily earthed.

He cannot touch her
for he fears to bruise what he longs
to worship
though he hungers for her hidden heart.

He would lay down his life for her
if he was not afraid
she might be mortal.

Airs Above the Ground

in the ballroom of sand
the lipizzaners are dancing to Bizet
a thousand crystals sparkling
in the patent-leather gleam of their hooves

a single stallion rises in capriole

aerial
he is a creature of light

The Tightrope Walker Presents Her Rose

She steps out onto the high wire,
no longer the leaping, bold steps of her youth,
but faltering,
tiny movements
slowed down
almost
to
stop.

Her costume sags,
bereft of its sparkling sequins
it is a dull shadow under the lights.
Against the fluffy white candy-floss of her hair
and faded blue of her eyes,
her blackened eyebrows startle.

She does not remember her routines;
her feet remember for her
and follow their own silent music.

Half-way across she pauses,
spreads feeble arms
and balances on one leg,
smiling as she acknowledges the applause,
the shouts of *bravo* and *encore*
that echo in her head.

She teeters for a moment;
with bemused expression continues;
in her hand, a red paper rose for her long gone love.

Voice in a Bell Jar
for Kerry

I have painted my beautiful girl
the colours of invisible,
taught her to walk silent through the world
as light through a prism.

With barbed wire and thorn
I have braided her silken hair;
in the moon's full light, placed a silver pentagram
on her milkycool brow.

With odour of leaf-mould I have disguised
the fragrance of her innocence,
chained to her small wrist a wolfhound
with jaws of steel.

But the life in her is stronger than all my defences;
around me and beyond me
she reaches for the world.

Would that the stone in my hand
were my heart made stone.

Woman in a Gondola

He longs to kiss her silken foot,
its instep arched like the Bridge of Sighs,
her face hidden behind a carnival mask,

or hold her satin shoe to his mouth
tenderly as a communion wafer,
his lips hungry for her fragrance of rose.

It would be enough for her to unfold
like a ripe fig in the sun-warmed night,
inviting lips to suck the dark red flesh
as though red were the only colour of love.

Watching her, he feels himself drawn
helpless as thread
through the eye of a needle.

An ordinary man
dreaming of a black swan.

Words Unspoken
for Ewan

My son's reflection in clear water
– face leaf-freckled,
eyes of indigo blue –
reaches out to me as though
it was an open hand
inviting me to step from solid ground
onto the spread of palm,
his smile telling me I can walk on water,
for wasn't that what I whispered
in his ear when he was a child at my side.

A sudden cloud across the sun
obscures his perfect reflection
and there is distance between us:

from the opposite bank of the stream
he watches me
and I wonder what we are to each other,
my son and I, and whether
the sun's light has made me transparent.

Looking across at him
I feel myself old and cold, a fish caught
on an invisible hook
hanging helpless in the current.

The cloud passes.
Silently he reaches out his hand,
his reflection
a slender bridge between us.

Picasso's Eyes

watch me as I move about the room.
The intensity of their gaze makes me awkward.
I drop a book,
pick it up, set it on the table,
casually push my hair off my face
and walk to the window
wondering which is my better side,
hating myself for my vanity.

His eyes are hands on my head
feeling the shape of my skull beneath my hair,
studying the planes and angles of my face,
the effect of the light upon my skin,
my reluctant body pliant to his touch.

I feel
deconstructed,
Dora Maar'd,

and I wonder if he will name me
Woman gazing self-consciously from a window,
Woman in a blue dress, tears in her eyes,
Woman I have taken to pieces and recreated
in the space of a minute.

Picasso's eyes watch me still.
I reach out and place his photograph face-down.

On a Cloud Formation at Achill

Cloud nuzzles mountain's neck,
biting into the tender flesh below her ear,
his hand resting on the curve of her waist,
a regular Romeo.
But he is fickle,
a shape-changer:
look at him now,
he's Humpty-Dumpty
perched on her upturned hip,
too cocky by far to take a fall.

Living Together

I want the space between us emptied of words,
swept out,
scrubbed clean
until nothing but silence remains.

Let us not be tempted to voice our history
or commit it to ink.
Let us leave the vellum unmarked,
its blank face potent as unspoken words.

I want our space shaped like an hourglass
so that however far apart we stand
our fingertips will always touch.

Let us not assume this is our journey through time
for our footsteps leave no trace
and the particles of sand in the hourglass
take no account of us.

I want this space the colour of rain
shot through with sunlight
for I was alone once and saw storm clouds
golden in the sun and I was held in that moment
unafraid.

Let us not be afraid;
fear makes us small and we need to be giants.

Above all
I want the mystery.

Let us never know each other too well.

Sole Song

Only his boots are visible,
unlaced;
the tongues are loose

and babble away to each other
about hard pavements, cold wet streets,
the price of a pint,

while he dreams
– cardboardboxed
in the piss and dirt of the subway floor –

of running barefoot on a sandy beach,
a double rum in the sun,
on ice,
with a straw
and a pink paper parasol;
of tumbling naked with the Wonderbra girl
on a bed of strawberries.

Nearby, a saxophonist
opens up on Otis Redding
and the tongues break into song.

On Bound Feet

she crosses the cobbled courtyard
willing herself to stumble
fall and shatter
all the pieces of herself to become dust
and be blown away on the wind.

Dragons emerge from the shadows,
their huge mouths stretched wide in silent roar.
Overhead, a dozen orange moons quiver
and she wonders if they too
are fearful of their fate.

Behind closed doors she hears
the voices of his other wives.
Sharp as knives
they cut her through and through
though she would trade places in an instant.

From child to wife quicker than an intake of breath.
Her heart is a moth fluttering helplessly
against the cage of her ribs.
She adjusts her heavy bridal robe;
a beautiful strait-jacket,
it prevents her taking flight.

In the opium haze of his bedroom
her husband dreams of feet smaller than lotus buds,
his toothless mouth hungry for their shape
and the porcelain-smooth body from which he will draw life.

It is time.
He opens the doors,
his old man's body trembling.

Victim

When I first saw you it was from a distance,
your body in that rain-soaked alley,
small, but too obviously human to be mistaken
for some tangle of rubbish discarded by a careless hand.

Your dress lay across your throat
and your nakedness stunned me,
made me tremble,
hesitate to come closer
but you drew me on

forced me to witness the frailty of your arms,
your exposed breasts,
your belly with its ancient stretch marks
and everywhere the livid scratches,
the beginnings of bruises.

It was so hard to look at your face,
your mouth frozen,
lips peeled back.
In my head I heard your screams
hammering on the back-yard doors,
each one closed tight against you.

Your eyes were open,
staring.
I could not bring myself to look into them,
afraid that I would see the face imprinted there;
afraid I would draw him to me.

Sisters

She pulls the pelt around her
and lies down in the winter cave
on a bed of moss.
Outside, driftwood is a tumble of bone
on the lakeshore,
the wind a low moan among pines.

Her breath barely stirs the silent air.
She feels herself no different
from the cave or the lake or the trees
and the darkness behind her eyes
is no more than the darkness around her.

She will already be dead when death comes.
No one will lay her out, wash her body clean
or perfume it with sacred oils.
No one will place the silver coin upon her tongue
or close her staring eyes.
No one will paint the history of her life
on the walls of the cave.
No one will mourn her.

Outside, a brown bear raises her head
and smells the air.

Trompe L'Oeil

Man Ray couldn't have arranged them
more artistically,
those tears on your cheeks;
tiny, perfect, pear-shaped.
They remind me of the pears ripening
on that window-sill in Moscow.
There is no name
for that colour of green,
you said, and *look,*
they are lined up
like a row of dissidents
about to be shot.

But these;
I imagine if I licked them off your skin
their hard, cold edges would cut my tongue
to pieces.

And then, my love, you open your eyes.

Snail-silver
for Deirdre McCrory

So delicate the shell,
the snail long gone,
no trace left of the froth and bubble
that signals movement
and turns into glide on stalks and leaves.

All is quiet inside the house;
if I could Alice-me-down-small
I would run along the curving hallway
to the inner chamber
still filled with the fragrance of fennel.
In the after-silence of snail,
I would fashion myself earrings
and toe-rings of silver.

Tattoo Me

A barbed braid around my waist
so that those who embrace me
cannot get too close.

A coiled snake around my throat
to remind me that I can shed my skin and be reborn
when love turns cold or treachery strikes.

Along the length of my spine, the moon ascending;
I was born in the sign of Scorpio
and night is when my spirit walks free.

On my left arm, my son with laughter in his eyes,
fear in his heart,
and on my right, my daughter, with her still unfelt pain.
When I hold myself
it will be my children holding me
and I can believe that they forgive me
for everything there is to forgive.

Let me not forget the faceless one,
unborn, unnamed,
he is the shadow that lies like a blade across my belly.

Tattoo pictures of childhood on my legs,
elves, goblins, witches,
the poisoned apple,
the transforming kiss.
On my left shoulder, a soaring eagle
for my dreams,
and on my right, a lead weight
to remind me of their burden.

All this, so that when I look in the mirror,
I will know who I am.

Nendrum Monastic Site

Broken at the knuckle
the round tower
rises silent amid the ruins
of an earlier community
and all around the sea flows silver.

Tread softly these concentric walls;
this site is sacred
to the vision that raised it stone on stone.

Names endure long after those
who gave them voice have ceased to be.
Here they prayed and talked,
sang and laughed
while all around the sea flowed silver.

But the words are gone.
Unroofed, they had no place to dwell.
I walk this ground in silence,
the only sound the ash keys stirring,
the past settling, lichen-light,
as all around the sea flows silver.

One Summer in Marseilles

A sudden flap of pigeons brings her, startled, to the window, to look out on a courtyard of spiralling feathers, breathless washing, and way up high, a tight-fitting lid of sky. Five o'clock and she is heat-drunk. Occasionally she goes to the door and listens for his footsteps on the stairs, but even the silence is silent.

A metal bedstead bangs frenetically against the wall of apartment six above. She imagines flying plaster, cockroaches scurrying for cover, an explosion of sweat-soaked sheets. In the after-silence she smells Gauloise and aches for the wet of love on her own skin. She cannot remember when she last felt love, cannot remember when he started reading her letters home and listening to her phone calls or when he first locked the door behind him as he left for work. She blames the heat, tells herself it has tricked her memory into remembering nothing and stolen her energy when her back was turned.

Midnight. The city snaps awake to wild African rhythms, the smell of hashish on the air. From her window she watches the men in their dark djellabahs crowding around the mouths of bars. Their laughter turns quickly and easily to violence and she has often watched it spill out onto the streets, a ballet with knives, choreographed to the scream of sirens that never come close.

Dawn. The heat is finally bearable. She lies naked on her bed, her hand fisted in the hollowed space his body used to fill.

She promises herself, today she will stop dreaming and will fly out of the window, home.

On the Red Sofa

She could be Anna Karenin sitting there
on the red sofa, her arm resting casually along its back,
a black Sobraine between her fingers.
Maybe it's her face; those grey eyes, intimate, distant,
the high cheekbones, the hint of cruelty
in those full lips the colour of crushed raspberries;
or maybe it's the half-light,
the worn red wallpaper behind her, glowing
with unorthodox depth against the room's dark shadows.

Look how she raises her wineglass to her lips
leaving just a whisper of lipstick on the rim,
and flicks her ash carelessly to the ground.
I imagine her holding court, a couple of Borzois at her feet,
a silver samovar bubbling away on a sideboard,
and somewhere in the background a cold, unyielding husband.
That young man standing there with adoration in his eyes
could be Vronsky about to fall to his knees before her,
her ring-heavy fingers pressed to his eager mouth.

Outside darkness has fallen.
Far away, trains rattle restlessly through the long northern night.

The Doorway

It must be van Gogh looking through my eyes
that causes my heart to race
as rooks and crows rise into the September sky,
bodies black against the insubstantial blue.

All is energy.

I close my eyes and feel their shadows
move across my eyelids
and it amazes me that shadows
hold the weight of feathered bodies.

If I could look through van Gogh's eyes,
perhaps shape and shadow would merge
revealing life itself
and sanity might not be too high a price to pay
for a glimpse of almighty beauty.

Crows and rooks riot in the air,
flight feathers spread.
I tell myself that somewhere
between shape and shadow is the doorway.

Congo

An old gorilla came to me in a dream,
fixed me with her carnelian eyes
and told me I would have a son
whose name would be Congo
for he would be mighty and strong
and would bring life to all around him.

I told her I already had two sons
whose names were Useless and Indolence.
My man, curse his sorry bones, had run off
leaving me scrabbling about in the dirt like a hen
for a few grains of food
and the only good thing in my life
was that my child-bearing days were over.

The old gorilla wrapped her hairy arms around me
and in the sharp tang of her sweat
it was as if the forest had drawn me to its centre
filling my nostrils with the pungency of earth and leaf-mould.
Deep in her chest the beat of her heart
was the waves pounding on the far-off shores of my childhood.
You will have a son, she said.

I saw myself fast asleep on my bed
while a strong wind blew
through the thin walls of my hut.
Round and around me the wind swirled and as I watched
it blew a tiny seed up into the barren waste of my womb
where it took root as though it had fallen on fertile ground.

When I awoke, my body felt washed in light
and I knew I was with child.
For nine months my belly grew big and round
and milk flowed from my abundant breasts.
My two hungry sons drank their fill and were reborn as men
with shoulders broad enough to bear the burdens of this life.
I renamed them Courageous and Brave and sent them out to work.

Came a day I walked into the forest,
slowly, for I was huge and heavy.
In a clearing I sat to watch the patterns
of light amongst the leaves,
and I felt her there, watching me from the trees,
still and immutable.
When she spoke, it could have been the voice of my soul.
His time has come.

I do not remember his birth, though I do remember
the forest coming alive with a beating of wings,
the singing of many birds,
a warm, tumultuous flow between my legs
as though a great river had sourced itself through me,
and all around the sharp scent of gorilla,
familiar to me as my own flesh.

I wandered in and out of sleep,
my dreams full of animals bringing me gifts of fruit and flowers
and I had no fear of the lions, snakes and wild pigs
that lay down about my feet.
When I awoke, it was in the arms of the old gorilla.
Where is my son? I asked her,
my belly and breasts are empty.

What is begun cannot be stopped, she said.
*Born out of the heart of darkness, his journey will take him
many lifetimes. He and his followers will swell the waters
of the ocean into a giant wave that will wash over the entire earth.
When the waters recede, the earth will be cleansed
and whole again, a new seed will take root,
and you and I will be the standing stones of an earlier age.*

Buried Alive

My body is slowly seizing up,
cell by cell,
limb by limb,
turning into stone.

They cannot tell me how it will end,
encephalitis lethargica.
I might be in the act of walking
or curled up in foetal position
which would make transportation easier
at least.

I seem to have been screaming forever.
No one hears me.
They crowd around,
stare into my eyes and touch me
as if I wasn't there.

There's talk of miracles.
They say I've healed the sick;
some even say I've raised the dead.
The stone angel they call me,
blessing my immobility,
kneeling before my outstretched hands.

I dream of hands,
hundreds of hands flocking around me like birds,
lifting my poor stone body to the cliff's edge
where they drop me onto the rocks below.

I hear my voice,
a glorious cry of freedom
bursting from the ruins of my mouth.

The Gift

She proffers it to him as a gift,
her finger in a small golden box,
perfect as a freshly cut tea-rose
there on the white linen tablecloth.

Gazing at it, he cannot recall the shape of her hands,
hidden now in their black lace gloves,
or their touch upon his skin.
Instead, he remembers the great wasteland of her bed
where she would press her finger to his lips
when she thought he might tell her of his past
and then claw at him
as though trying to tear out his heart
before falling back, exhausted, her face wet with tears.

Now this.
Her gift to unseal his lips.

A chill wind blows through the restaurant.
Outside the sky darkens for rain.
Invisible barbs press into his flesh
reminding him
that although he has survived, he has no hope of escape.

As if he could ever tell her he has no heart to give her,
that he is a hollow man
seeing only death's head in her beautiful face
and in her firm scented flesh
an emaciated body, cold and lifeless,
the taste of ashes bitter to the tongue.

Nocturne

It is so right that you should play Chopin
at this time of evening,
the shadows long across the grass,
buttercups beginning to close their petals
against the night.

The music fills the house and spills out into the garden;
it is the play of light in water,
the arabesque of swallows,
and each note played
leaves a soft indentation in my memory.

When the last notes fade into silence
it is not just the absence of music,
it is you at your piano,
your face rapt,
Chopin alive in your fingers.